M000087044

Fun-Flap Math
Fractions & Decimals

by Liane B. Onish

NEW YORK • TORONTO • LONDON • AUCKLAND • SYDNEY
MEXICO CITY • NEW DELHI • HONG KONG • BUENOS AIRES

Teaching
Resources

Hi Mom!

Thanks to Deborah Schecter, Mackie Rhodes,
and to everyone who contributed to this book.

Text on pages 4–6 adapted from *Fun-Flap Facts: Multiplication* by Danielle Blood.
Copyright © 2004 by Danielle Blood. Used by permission of Scholastic Teaching Resources.

Scholastic Inc. grants teachers permission to photocopy the reproducible pages in this book for classroom use. No other part of this publication may be reproduced in whole or in part, or stored in a retrieval system, or transmitted in any form or by any means, electronic, photocopying, recording, or otherwise, without written permission of the publisher. For information regarding permission, write to Scholastic Inc., 557 Broadway, New York, NY 10012-3999.

Written by Liane B. Onish
Edited by Immacula A. Rhodes
Cover design by Maria Lilja
Interior illustrations by Teresa Anderko
Interior design by Kathy Massaro

ISBN-13: 978-0-545-20927-4
ISBN-10: 0-545-20927-7

Text and illustrations © 2010 by Scholastic Inc.
All rights reserved. Published by Scholastic Inc.
Printed in the U.S.A.

2 3 4 5 6 7 8 9 10   40   17 16 15 14 13 12 11

Contents

Introduction

Welcome to *Fun-Flap Math: Fractions & Decimals*, a hands-on way to help students practice essential math skills. This book includes 32 reproducible fun flaps that feature the same interactive format that students know and love. Fun flaps are ideal for learning centers or for use during transition times—in the morning, before or after lunch, at the end of the day, or for practice at home.

Each fun flap features eight problems. Students read and answer the problem, then lift the flap to reveal the answer and a challenge problem. You'll also find additional reproducible pages to make using the fun flaps even easier:

* step-by-step directions for folding the fun flaps (page 6)
* a checklist to help students keep track of the fun flaps they've done (page 7)
* self-checking quizzes that let students check their progress and write their scores as both fractions and percentages (pages 8–15)
* a fun flap template for students to make their own fun flaps (page 48)

The engaging format and humorous illustrations encourage students to review skills again and again. Mastering fractions, decimals, and percents has never been so much fun!

How to Use This Book

There are many ways these fun flaps can be used in the classroom and at home. Here are some teaching tips to get started.

* Make copies of the fun flaps, store them in labeled hanging files, and place these in a learning center. After demonstrating how to fold the fun flaps, post the folding directions nearby. (Many students know how to fold these, but the directions will guide them if questions arise.)

* Have students decorate individualized pocket folders to use for storing their fun flaps, checklists, and quizzes. Explain how to use the checklist to keep track of which fun flaps students have used and to record their quiz scores.

* Brainstorm with students a list of ways that they might use the fun flaps to support a productive environment in the classroom—for example, speaking in low voices when reading and answering the questions.

* Introduce a new fun flap each week. Write the number and title of the fun flap on a sheet of art paper. Draw or list concept reminders, for example, draw several different shapes and divide them into halves, thirds, quarters, and so on. Then label the sections of each shape with the corresponding fractional parts.

* After working with each fun flap, ask students to cut out the self-checking quiz and fold over the right side to cover the answers. Have them answer the problems and check their work. Then show students how to record their quiz scores as fractions and percentages on the checklist.

Using the Fun Flaps

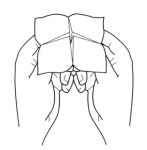

1 Partner A holds the fun flap in a closed position, so that the points touch. Partner A asks Partner B to choose a picture on a flap.

2 Partner B selects one of the four pictures.

3 Partner A opens and closes the fun flap the number of times shown above the selected picture, ending with the fun flap in an open position. Partner A holds the fun flap so Partner B can view the four problems.

4 Partner B chooses a problem and solves it. Partner A lifts the flap to reveal the answer and reads aloud the challenge beneath the flap.

5 Partners can switch roles at any point. Practice continues until both partners have taken several turns and are familiar with all eight problems on the fun flap.

Fun Flap Folding Directions

1 Trim off the top part of the fun flap page.

2 Place the fun flap on a flat surface with the blank side facing up.

3 Fold back the four corners along the solid lines so that they touch in the center of the square.

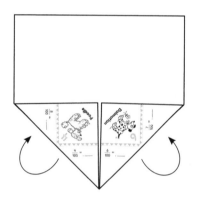

4 Turn over the fun flap. Fold back the corners again so that they touch the center of the square.

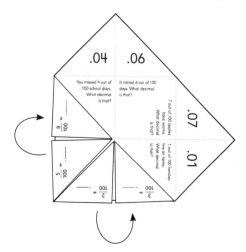

5 Fold the fun flap in half.

6 Place your right thumb and index finger in the right side.

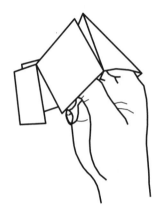

7 Place your left thumb and index finger in the left side.

8 Open and close the fun flap by moving your fingers.

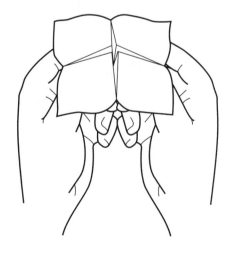

Fun-Flap Math: Fractions & Decimals © 2010 by Liane B. Onish, Scholastic Teaching Resources

Name _____

Fun Flap
Checklist

Mark an X under "Fun Flap Practice" after you have practiced with the fun flap.
Record your quiz score as a fraction and percent (such as $\frac{9}{10}$ and 90%).

Fun Flap	Fun Flap Practice	Quiz Score	
		Fraction	%
1 Pizza! (identifying fractions)			
2 On the Nose (identifying fractions)			
3 Strange Quartet (finding equivalent fractions)			
4 Egg-Xactly! (renaming fractions in lowest terms)			
5 Bakery Bites (comparing fractions)			
6 Up, Up, and Away (comparing mixed numbers)			
7 Brrr! (comparing mixed numbers)			
8 Fruity Flavors (renaming improper fractions as whole numbers)			
9 Book It! (renaming improper fractions as mixed numbers)			
10 Looking Up (renaming mixed numbers as improper fractions)			
11 Spring Flowers (adding fractions)			
12 It's Only Myth Believe (subtracting fractions)			
13 Play Ball! (adding mixed numbers)			
14 Creepy Crawlies (subtracting mixed numbers)			
15 Top It Off (adding and subtracting mixed numbers)			
16 Get on Board! (renaming fractions as decimals: tenths place)			
17 Dog Days (renaming fractions as decimals: hundredths place)			
18 Indoor Sports (renaming mixed numbers as decimals: tenths)			
19 Black and White (renaming mixed numbers as decimals: hundredths)			
20 Awesome Outings (comparing decimals)			
21 Time With Friends (adding decimals: tenths)			
22 Sea Scene (adding decimals: hundredths)			
23 Cats Can (adding decimals: money)			
24 Just Relax (subtracting decimals: tenths)			
25 Art Attack! (subtracting decimals: hundredths)			
26 Shells to Go (subtracting decimals: money)			
27 Desert Life (renaming fractions as percentages)			
28 Whee! (renaming fractions as percentages)			
29 Super Seasons (renaming decimals as percentages)			
30 Let's Go Shopping (finding 50% of dollar amounts)			
31 Don't Rock the Boat! (finding percentages of $10.00)			
32 Fantastic Fair Food (finding percentages of dollar amounts)			

Fractions — rows 1–15
Decimals — rows 16–26
Percents — rows 27–32

Fun-Flap Math: Fractions & Decimals © 2010 by Liane B. Onish, Scholastic Teaching Resources

Name _____ Date _____

What fraction of each shape is shaded?

1.   2. (circle)

3. (circle)   4. (circle)

5. (circle)   6. (circle)

7. (circle)   8. (circle)

9. (circle)   10. (circle)

1. _____

2. _____

3. _____

4. _____

5. _____

6. _____

7. _____

8. _____

9. _____

10. _____

Fold here.

$\frac{1}{2}$

$\frac{2}{3}$

$\frac{3}{4}$

$\frac{2}{5}$

$\frac{2}{6}$

$\frac{3}{8}$

$\frac{4}{9}$

$\frac{5}{10}$

$\frac{5}{6}$

$\frac{1}{4}$

Name _____ Date _____

What fraction of each shape is shaded?

1.   2.

3. (square)   4. (rectangle)

5.   6.

7.   8.

9. (rectangle)   10. (rectangle)

1. _____

2. _____

3. _____

4. _____

5. _____

6. _____

7. _____

8. _____

9. _____

10. _____

Fold here.

$\frac{1}{3}$

$\frac{4}{5}$

$\frac{1}{4}$

$\frac{5}{8}$

$\frac{8}{10}$

$\frac{2}{7}$

$\frac{4}{9}$

$\frac{3}{6}$

$\frac{3}{5}$

$\frac{3}{4}$

Name _____ Date _____

Find the equivalent fractions.

1. $\frac{1}{2} = \frac{\square}{4}$ 2. $\frac{4}{8} = \frac{1}{\square}$

3. $\frac{2}{6} = \frac{1}{\square}$ 4. $\frac{3}{4} = \frac{\square}{8}$

5. $\frac{6}{9} = \frac{\square}{3}$ 6. $\frac{9}{12} = \frac{3}{\square}$

7. $\frac{4}{10} = \frac{\square}{5}$ 8. $\frac{1}{4} = \frac{2}{\square}$

9. $\frac{3}{5} = \frac{\square}{10}$ 10. $\frac{2}{3} = \frac{4}{\square}$

1. _____

2. _____

3. _____

4. _____

5. _____

6. _____

7. _____

8. _____

9. _____

10. _____

Fold here.

$\frac{2}{4}$

$\frac{1}{2}$

$\frac{1}{3}$

$\frac{6}{8}$

$\frac{2}{3}$

$\frac{3}{4}$

$\frac{2}{5}$

$\frac{2}{8}$

$\frac{6}{10}$

$\frac{4}{6}$

Name _____ Date _____

Find the equivalent fractions.

1. $\frac{4}{8} = \frac{\square}{2}$ 2. $\frac{4}{6} = \frac{\square}{3}$

3. $\frac{9}{12} = \frac{\square}{4}$ 4. $\frac{3}{24} = \frac{\square}{8}$

5. $\frac{3}{9} = \frac{1}{\square}$ 6. $\frac{4}{10} = \frac{2}{\square}$

7. $\frac{6}{16} = \frac{3}{\square}$ 8. $\frac{4}{16} = \frac{1}{\square}$

9. $\frac{10}{12} = \frac{5}{\square}$ 10. $\frac{3}{12} = \frac{1}{\square}$

1. _____

2. _____

3. _____

4. _____

5. _____

6. _____

7. _____

8. _____

9. _____

10. _____

Fold here.

$\frac{1}{2}$

$\frac{2}{3}$

$\frac{3}{4}$

$\frac{1}{8}$

$\frac{1}{3}$

$\frac{2}{5}$

$\frac{3}{8}$

$\frac{1}{4}$

$\frac{5}{6}$

$\frac{1}{4}$

5

Name _____ Date _____

Which fraction is greater? Circle the answer.

1.	$\frac{1}{4}$	$\frac{1}{5}$		$\frac{1}{4}$
2.	$\frac{4}{6}$	$\frac{3}{4}$		$\frac{3}{4}$
3.	$\frac{1}{4}$	$\frac{3}{8}$		$\frac{3}{8}$
4.	$\frac{3}{6}$	$\frac{1}{3}$		$\frac{3}{6}$
5.	$\frac{2}{8}$	$\frac{2}{4}$		$\frac{2}{4}$
6.	$\frac{1}{2}$	$\frac{1}{3}$		$\frac{1}{2}$
7.	$\frac{2}{10}$	$\frac{3}{5}$		$\frac{3}{5}$
8.	$\frac{1}{4}$	$\frac{5}{8}$		$\frac{5}{8}$
9.	$\frac{1}{5}$	$\frac{1}{3}$		$\frac{1}{3}$
10.	$\frac{1}{6}$	$\frac{2}{9}$		$\frac{2}{9}$

Fold here.

6

Name _____ Date _____

Which mixed number is greater? Circle the answer.

1.	$1\frac{3}{4}$	$1\frac{1}{2}$		$1\frac{3}{4}$
2.	$4\frac{1}{4}$	$4\frac{5}{12}$		$4\frac{5}{12}$
3.	$2\frac{5}{8}$	$2\frac{1}{2}$		$2\frac{5}{8}$
4.	$1\frac{2}{8}$	$1\frac{3}{16}$		$1\frac{2}{8}$
5.	$2\frac{1}{4}$	$2\frac{3}{8}$		$2\frac{3}{8}$
6.	$3\frac{3}{5}$	$3\frac{1}{10}$		$3\frac{3}{5}$
7.	$3\frac{4}{6}$	$3\frac{1}{3}$		$3\frac{4}{6}$
8.	$2\frac{2}{3}$	$2\frac{10}{12}$		$2\frac{10}{12}$
9.	$1\frac{3}{8}$	$1\frac{1}{4}$		$1\frac{3}{8}$
10.	$2\frac{1}{3}$	$2\frac{1}{8}$		$2\frac{1}{3}$

Fold here.

7

Name _____ Date _____

Which mixed number is greater? Circle the answer.

1.	$2\frac{1}{4}$	$2\frac{3}{8}$		$2\frac{3}{8}$
2.	$3\frac{2}{3}$	$3\frac{1}{16}$		$3\frac{2}{3}$
3.	$1\frac{3}{10}$	$1\frac{1}{5}$		$1\frac{3}{10}$
4.	$2\frac{5}{8}$	$2\frac{5}{16}$		$2\frac{5}{8}$
5.	$3\frac{1}{2}$	$3\frac{7}{10}$		$3\frac{7}{10}$
6.	$2\frac{5}{12}$	$2\frac{1}{2}$		$2\frac{1}{2}$
7.	$1\frac{3}{4}$	$1\frac{1}{3}$		$1\frac{3}{4}$
8.	$4\frac{1}{8}$	$4\frac{3}{16}$		$4\frac{3}{16}$
9.	$2\frac{1}{3}$	$2\frac{1}{4}$		$2\frac{1}{3}$
10.	$3\frac{5}{6}$	$3\frac{3}{4}$		$3\frac{5}{6}$

Fold here.

8

Name _____ Date _____

Write each improper fraction as a whole number.

1.	$\frac{10}{2}$	_____	5
2.	$\frac{18}{6}$	_____	3
3.	$\frac{30}{5}$	_____	6
4.	$\frac{14}{7}$	_____	2
5.	$\frac{16}{4}$	_____	4
6.	$\frac{24}{3}$	_____	8
7.	$\frac{21}{3}$	_____	7
8.	$\frac{12}{12}$	_____	1
9.	$\frac{18}{2}$	_____	9
10.	$\frac{9}{3}$	_____	3

Fold here.

Name _____ Date _____

Write each improper fraction as a mixed number.

1. $\frac{10}{4}$ _____ $2\frac{2}{4}$

2. $\frac{11}{6}$ _____ $1\frac{5}{6}$

3. $\frac{20}{9}$ _____ $2\frac{2}{9}$

4. $\frac{13}{3}$ _____ $4\frac{1}{3}$

5. $\frac{15}{2}$ _____ $7\frac{1}{2}$

6. $\frac{8}{5}$ _____ $1\frac{3}{5}$

7. $\frac{17}{7}$ _____ $2\frac{3}{7}$

8. $\frac{20}{8}$ _____ $2\frac{4}{8}$

9. $\frac{7}{6}$ _____ $1\frac{1}{6}$

10. $\frac{11}{3}$ _____ $3\frac{2}{3}$

Fold here.

Name _____ Date _____

Write each mixed number as an improper fraction.

1. $1\frac{1}{3}$ _____ $\frac{4}{3}$

2. $2\frac{4}{5}$ _____ $\frac{14}{5}$

3. $1\frac{3}{8}$ _____ $\frac{11}{8}$

4. $3\frac{1}{4}$ _____ $\frac{13}{4}$

5. $4\frac{1}{2}$ _____ $\frac{9}{2}$

6. $2\frac{2}{3}$ _____ $\frac{8}{3}$

7. $3\frac{3}{4}$ _____ $\frac{15}{4}$

8. $2\frac{5}{8}$ _____ $\frac{21}{8}$

9. $9\frac{1}{2}$ _____ $\frac{19}{2}$

10. $3\frac{1}{3}$ _____ $\frac{10}{3}$

Fold here.

Name _____ Date _____

Solve each problem.

1. $\frac{1}{3} + \frac{1}{3} =$ _____ $\frac{2}{3}$

2. $\frac{1}{4} + \frac{2}{4} =$ _____ $\frac{3}{4}$

3. $\frac{3}{5} + \frac{1}{5} =$ _____ $\frac{4}{5}$

4. $\frac{4}{10} + \frac{5}{10} =$ _____ $\frac{9}{10}$

5. $\frac{2}{7} + \frac{3}{7} =$ _____ $\frac{5}{7}$

6. $\frac{3}{8} + \frac{4}{8} =$ _____ $\frac{7}{8}$

7. $\frac{1}{6} + \frac{3}{6} =$ _____ $\frac{4}{6}$

8. $\frac{2}{9} + \frac{4}{9} =$ _____ $\frac{6}{9}$

9. $\frac{3}{12} + \frac{4}{12} =$ _____ $\frac{7}{12}$

10. $\frac{1}{9} + \frac{4}{9} =$ _____ $\frac{5}{9}$

Fold here.

Name _____ Date _____

Solve each problem.

1. $\frac{2}{3} - \frac{1}{3} =$ _____ $\frac{1}{3}$

2. $\frac{3}{4} - \frac{2}{4} =$ _____ $\frac{1}{4}$

3. $\frac{3}{5} - \frac{1}{5} =$ _____ $\frac{2}{5}$

4. $\frac{5}{10} - \frac{1}{10} =$ _____ $\frac{4}{10}$

5. $\frac{4}{8} - \frac{2}{8} =$ _____ $\frac{2}{8}$

6. $\frac{8}{9} - \frac{3}{9} =$ _____ $\frac{5}{9}$

7. $\frac{10}{12} - \frac{4}{12} =$ _____ $\frac{6}{12}$

8. $\frac{5}{6} - \frac{2}{6} =$ _____ $\frac{3}{6}$

9. $\frac{4}{5} - \frac{2}{5} =$ _____ $\frac{2}{5}$

10. $\frac{6}{7} - \frac{3}{7} =$ _____ $\frac{3}{7}$

Fold here.

13

Name _____ Date _____

Solve each problem.

1. $1\frac{1}{4} + 2\frac{1}{4} =$ _____ $3\frac{2}{4}$

2. $2\frac{2}{8} + 3\frac{3}{8} =$ _____ $5\frac{5}{8}$

3. $3\frac{1}{5} + 1\frac{3}{5} =$ _____ $4\frac{4}{5}$

4. $2\frac{2}{6} + 4\frac{3}{6} =$ _____ $6\frac{5}{6}$

5. $4\frac{3}{7} + 4\frac{1}{7} =$ _____ $8\frac{4}{7}$

6. $10\frac{1}{3} + 4\frac{1}{3} =$ _____ $14\frac{2}{3}$

7. $7\frac{1}{4} + 6\frac{2}{4} =$ _____ $13\frac{3}{4}$

8. $5\frac{2}{9} + 6\frac{3}{9} =$ _____ $11\frac{5}{9}$

9. $1\frac{2}{5} + 5\frac{2}{5} =$ _____ $6\frac{4}{5}$

10. $2\frac{3}{8} + 7\frac{4}{8} =$ _____ $9\frac{7}{8}$

Fold here.

14

Name _____ Date _____

Solve each problem.

1. $2\frac{3}{4} - 1\frac{1}{4} =$ _____ $1\frac{2}{4}$

2. $5\frac{2}{3} - 1\frac{1}{3} =$ _____ $4\frac{1}{3}$

3. $6\frac{5}{8} - 2\frac{2}{8} =$ _____ $4\frac{3}{8}$

4. $8\frac{5}{6} - 2\frac{1}{6} =$ _____ $6\frac{4}{6}$

5. $7\frac{3}{4} - 2\frac{2}{4} =$ _____ $5\frac{1}{4}$

6. $12\frac{7}{10} - 5\frac{2}{10} =$ _____ $7\frac{5}{10}$

7. $4\frac{1}{2} - 1 =$ _____ $3\frac{1}{2}$

8. $10\frac{7}{9} - 2\frac{5}{9} =$ _____ $8\frac{2}{9}$

9. $6\frac{4}{6} - 1\frac{3}{6} =$ _____ $5\frac{1}{6}$

10. $2\frac{7}{9} - \frac{2}{9} =$ _____ $2\frac{5}{9}$

Fold here.

15

Name _____ Date _____

Solve each problem.

1. $5\frac{2}{5} + 1\frac{1}{5} =$ _____ $6\frac{3}{5}$

2. $2\frac{1}{4} + 5\frac{2}{4} =$ _____ $7\frac{3}{4}$

3. $12\frac{11}{12} - 3\frac{2}{12} =$ _____ $9\frac{9}{12}$

4. $10\frac{6}{7} - 7\frac{1}{7} =$ _____ $3\frac{5}{7}$

5. $6\frac{5}{8} + 2\frac{2}{8} =$ _____ $8\frac{7}{8}$

6. $2\frac{5}{6} - 1\frac{1}{6} =$ _____ $1\frac{4}{6}$

7. $8\frac{3}{9} - 3\frac{2}{9} =$ _____ $5\frac{1}{9}$

8. $1\frac{2}{10} + 3\frac{3}{10} =$ _____ $4\frac{5}{10}$

9. $7\frac{6}{8} - 4\frac{3}{8} =$ _____ $3\frac{3}{8}$

10. $4\frac{6}{11} + 1\frac{3}{11} =$ _____ $5\frac{9}{11}$

Fold here.

16

Name _____ Date _____

Write each fraction as a decimal to the tenth place.

1. $\frac{3}{10}$ _____   .3

2. $\frac{7}{10}$ _____   .7

3. $\frac{5}{10}$ _____   .5

4. $\frac{1}{10}$ _____   .1

5. $\frac{2}{10}$ _____   .2

6. $\frac{8}{10}$ _____   .8

7. $\frac{4}{10}$ _____   .4

8. $\frac{6}{10}$ _____   .6

9. $\frac{1}{5}$ _____   .2

10. $\frac{4}{5}$ _____   .8

Fold here.

17

Name _____ Date _____

Write each fraction as a decimal to the hundredth place.

1. $\frac{5}{100}$ _____ .05

2. $\frac{2}{100}$ _____ .02

3. $\frac{8}{100}$ _____ .08

4. $\frac{4}{100}$ _____ .04

5. $\frac{3}{100}$ _____ .03

6. $\frac{1}{100}$ _____ .01

7. $\frac{6}{100}$ _____ .06

8. $\frac{7}{100}$ _____ .07

9. $\frac{2}{50}$ _____ .04

10. $\frac{4}{50}$ _____ .08

Fold here.

18

Name _____ Date _____

Write each mixed number as a decimal.

1. $1\frac{2}{10}$ _____ 1.2

2. $3\frac{6}{10}$ _____ 3.6

3. $2\frac{8}{10}$ _____ 2.8

4. $4\frac{7}{10}$ _____ 4.7

5. $9\frac{1}{10}$ _____ 9.1

6. $11\frac{4}{10}$ _____ 11.4

7. $8\frac{9}{10}$ _____ 8.9

8. $12\frac{3}{10}$ _____ 12.3

9. $6\frac{5}{10}$ _____ 6.5

10. $5\frac{8}{10}$ _____ 5.8

Fold here.

19

Name _____ Date _____

Write each mixed number as a decimal.

1. $2\frac{8}{100}$ _____ 2.08

2. $1\frac{3}{100}$ _____ 1.03

3. $3\frac{5}{100}$ _____ 3.05

4. $4\frac{2}{100}$ _____ 4.02

5. $10\frac{9}{100}$ _____ 10.09

6. $12\frac{6}{100}$ _____ 12.06

7. $9\frac{7}{100}$ _____ 9.07

8. $8\frac{4}{100}$ _____ 8.04

9. $5\frac{1}{100}$ _____ 5.01

10. $7\frac{6}{100}$ _____ 7.06

Fold here.

20

Name _____ Date _____

Which number is greater? Circle the answer.

1.	2	1.02	2
2.	4.06	4.6	4.6
3.	3.7	3.07	3.7
4.	9.6	9.06	9.6
5.	12.05	12.5	12.5
6.	1.03	1.3	1.3
7.	4.8	4.08	4.8
8.	6.05	6.5	6.5
9.	8.1	8.01	8.1
10.	6.04	6.4	6.4

Fold here.

21

Name _____ Date _____

Solve each problem.

1. $1.2 + 1.5 =$ _____   2.7

2. $2.3 + 4.1 =$ _____   6.4

3. $3.5 + 2.3 =$ _____   5.8

4. $4.4 + 5.5 =$ _____   9.9

5. $3.1 + 4.2 =$ _____   7.3

6. $2.2 + 2.3 =$ _____   4.5

7. $2.5 + 1.1 =$ _____   3.6

8. $3.1 + 3.1 =$ _____   6.2

9. $6.4 + 1.3 =$ _____   7.7

10. $5.2 + 0.5 =$ _____   5.7

Fold here.

22

Name _____ Date _____

Solve each problem.

1. $1.02 + 2.50 =$ _____   3.52

2. $2.30 + 4.11 =$ _____   6.41

3. $3.25 + 5.52 =$ _____   8.77

4. $4.14 + 5.25 =$ _____   9.39

5. $3.10 + 4.03 =$ _____   7.13

6. $5.17 + 1.10 =$ _____   6.27

7. $2.45 + 3.23 =$ _____   5.68

8. $3.12 + 7.12 =$ _____   10.24

9. $9.39 + 0.01 =$ _____   9.40

10. $5.64 + 1.23 =$ _____   6.87

Fold here.

23

Name _____ Date _____

Solve each problem.

1. $\$1.25 + \$1.20 =$ _____ $2.45

2. $\$2.10 + \$3.08 =$ _____ $5.18

3. $\$3.89 + \$1.10 =$ _____ $4.99

4. $\$4.40 + \$5.47 =$ _____ $9.87

5. $\$1.52 + \$2.02 =$ _____ $3.54

6. $\$4.23 + \$1.53 =$ _____ $5.76

7. $\$2.31 + \$2.30 =$ _____ $4.61

8. $\$5.10 + \$3.10 =$ _____ $8.20

9. $\$5.18 + \$1.82 =$ _____ $7.00

10. $\$4.50 + \$0.11 =$ _____ $4.61

Fold here.

24

Name _____ Date _____

Solve each problem.

1. $2.7 - 1.5 =$ _____   1.2

2. $6.5 - 2.1 =$ _____   4.4

3. $9.9 - 4.2 =$ _____   5.7

4. $8.8 - 2.5 =$ _____   6.3

5. $9.7 - 1.1 =$ _____   8.6

6. $5.7 - 2.2 =$ _____   3.5

7. $8.2 - 1.1 =$ _____   7.1

8. $3.9 - 1.2 =$ _____   2.7

9. $1.9 - 0.4 =$ _____   1.5

10. $8.6 - 7.1 =$ _____   1.5

Fold here.

25

Name _____ Date _____

Solve each problem.

1. $6.50 - 2.20 =$ _____ 4.30
2. $3.96 - 1.50 =$ _____ 2.46
3. $7.31 - 4.11 =$ _____ 3.20
4. $6.52 - 1.51 =$ _____ 5.01
5. $9.25 - 3.20 =$ _____ 6.05
6. $4.30 - 2.10 =$ _____ 2.20
7. $5.17 - 1.10 =$ _____ 4.07
8. $3.45 - 1.23 =$ _____ 2.22
9. $4.90 - 2.25 =$ _____ 2.65
10. $2.07 - 1.07 =$ _____ 1.00

26

Name _____ Date _____

Solve each problem.

1. $\$2.50 - \$1.00 =$ _____ $1.50
2. $\$6.59 - \$2.11 =$ _____ $4.48
3. $\$9.96 - \$4.23 =$ _____ $5.73
4. $\$8.18 - \$2.14 =$ _____ $6.04
5. $\$9.35 - \$5.05 =$ _____ $4.30
6. $\$5.27 - \$2.26 =$ _____ $3.01
7. $\$8.25 - \$1.10 =$ _____ $7.15
8. $\$3.99 - \$1.17 =$ _____ $2.82
9. $\$6.00 - \$5.73 =$ _____ $0.27
10. $\$2.82 - \$0.75 =$ _____ $2.07

27

Name _____ Date _____

What fraction and percentage of each shape is shaded?

1. _____ _____% $\frac{4}{10}$, 40%
2. _____ _____% $\frac{2}{10}$, 20%
3. _____ _____% $\frac{6}{10}$, 60%
4. _____ _____% $\frac{3}{10}$, 30%
5. _____ _____% $\frac{7}{10}$, 70%
6. _____ _____% $\frac{1}{10}$, 10%
7. _____ _____% $\frac{8}{10}$, 80%
8. _____ _____% $\frac{5}{10}$, 50%
9. _____ _____% $\frac{10}{10}$, 100%
10. _____ _____% $\frac{9}{10}$, 90%

28

Name _____ Date _____

Write a fraction in its lowest term for each shaded part. Then write the fraction as a percent.

1. _____ _____% $\frac{1}{2}$, 50%
2. _____ _____% $\frac{1}{2}$, 50%
3. _____ _____% $\frac{1}{4}$, 25%
4. _____ _____% $\frac{1}{2}$, 50%
5. _____ _____% $\frac{3}{4}$, 75%
6. _____ _____% $\frac{1}{4}$, 25%
7. _____ _____% $\frac{1}{4}$, 25%
8. _____ _____% $\frac{3}{4}$, 75%
9. _____ _____% $\frac{1}{4}$, 25%
10. _____ _____% $\frac{1}{2}$, 50%

29

Name _____ Date _____

Write each decimal as a percent.

1.	.80	_____	80%
2.	.75	_____	75%
3.	.48	_____	48%
4.	.52	_____	52%
5.	.96	_____	96%
6.	.39	_____	39%
7.	.21	_____	21%
8.	.63	_____	63%
9.	.25	_____	25%
10.	.15	_____	15%

Fold here.

30

Name _____ Date _____

Find 50% of each amount.

1.	$3.00	_____	$1.50
2.	$6.00	_____	$3.00
3.	$100.00	_____	$50.00
4.	$9.00	_____	$4.50
5.	$32.00	_____	$16.00
6.	$24.00	_____	$12.00
7.	$2.00	_____	$1.00
8.	$8.00	_____	$4.00
9.	$40.00	_____	$20.00
10.	$15.00	_____	$7.50

Fold here.

31

Name _____ Date _____

Find the percentage of each amount.

1.	70%	of $10.00	_____	$7.00
2.	10%	of $10.00	_____	$1.00
3.	30%	of $10.00	_____	$3.00
4.	50%	of $10.00	_____	$5.00
5.	40%	of $10.00	_____	$4.00
6.	60%	of $10.00	_____	$6.00
7.	20%	of $10.00	_____	$2.00
8.	90%	of $10.00	_____	$9.00
9.	80%	of $10.00	_____	$8.00
10.	100%	of $10.00	_____	$10.00

Fold here.

32

Name _____ Date _____

Find the percentage of each amount.

1.	50%	of $12.00	_____	$6.00
2.	20%	of $50.00	_____	$10.00
3.	40%	of $20.00	_____	$8.00
4.	90%	of $10.00	_____	$9.00
5.	30%	of $60.00	_____	$18.00
6.	60%	of $100.00	_____	$60.00
7.	10%	of $10.00	_____	$1.00
8.	80%	of $20.00	_____	$16.00
9.	50%	of $6.00	_____	$3.00
10.	30%	of $30.00	_____	$9.00

Fold here.

1 Pizza!

What fraction of each circle is shaded?
Pick your favorite pizza to start.

cheese pizza

2

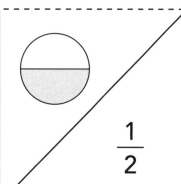

$\frac{1}{2}$

$\frac{3}{4}$

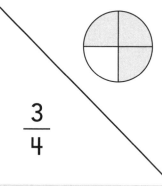

pepperoni pizza

3

Name the letters in
the first half of the
alphabet.

Sue played $\frac{3}{4}$ of a
game. What fraction
did she not play?

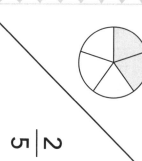

$\frac{2}{3}$

What is the
numerator of $\frac{2}{3}$?

You ate $\frac{2}{5}$ of a pizza.
What fraction
is left?

$\frac{2}{5}$

$\frac{2}{6}$

Would you rather have
$\frac{1}{3}$ or $\frac{2}{6}$ of a pizza?
Explain.

A team has 9 players.
How many players
make $\frac{4}{9}$ of the
team?

$\frac{4}{9}$

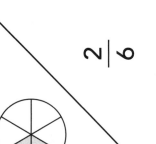

3 of your 8 favorite
foods are red. Name
the fraction.

Wiggle $\frac{5}{10}$ of
your toes.

veggie pizza

4

$\frac{3}{8}$

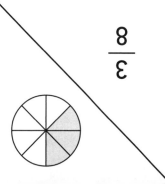

$\frac{5}{10}$

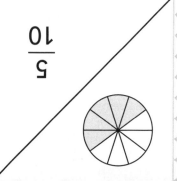

mushroom pizza

5

2 On the Nose

What fraction of each shape is shaded?
Pick your favorite sea lion act to start.

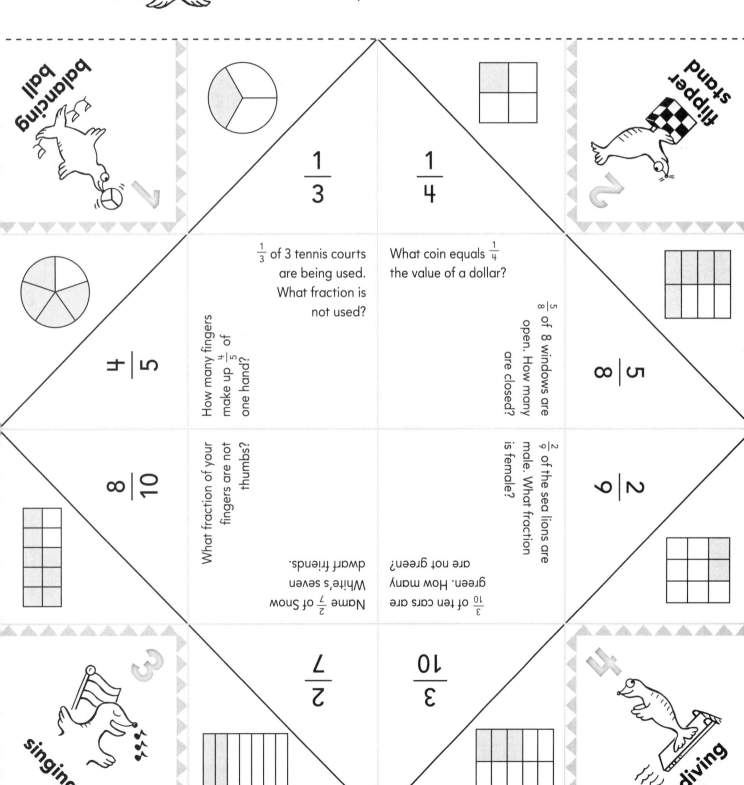

balancing ball 1

flipper stand 2

singing 3

diving 4

$\frac{1}{3}$

$\frac{1}{4}$

$\frac{4}{5}$

$\frac{5}{8}$

$\frac{8}{10}$

$\frac{2}{9}$

$\frac{2}{7}$

$\frac{3}{10}$

$\frac{1}{3}$ of 3 tennis courts are being used. What fraction is not used?

What coin equals $\frac{1}{4}$ the value of a dollar?

How many fingers make up $\frac{4}{5}$ of one hand?

$\frac{5}{8}$ of 8 windows are open. How many are closed?

What fraction of your fingers are not thumbs?

$\frac{2}{9}$ of the sea lions are male. What fraction is female?

Name $\frac{2}{7}$ of Snow White's seven dwarf friends.

$\frac{3}{10}$ of ten cars are green. How many are not green?

3 Strange Quartet

Name the equivalent fractions.
Pick your favorite stringed instrument to start.

cello

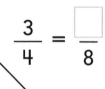

guitar

$\dfrac{1}{2} = \dfrac{\square}{4}$

$\dfrac{2}{4}$

$\dfrac{1}{3}$

$\dfrac{2}{6} = \dfrac{1}{\square}$

$\dfrac{4}{8} = \dfrac{1}{\square}$

Name $\dfrac{2}{4}$ of the cello's strings: A, D, G, C.

$\dfrac{2}{3}$ of the 3 guitarists are lefties. How many are righties?

$\dfrac{3}{4} = \dfrac{\square}{8}$

$\dfrac{1}{2}$

$\dfrac{1}{2}$ of the 8 musicians sit. How many stand?

The band played $\dfrac{3}{4}$ of their 8 songs. They will play ____ more.

$\dfrac{6}{8}$

$\dfrac{2}{3}$

6 of the 9 harp players are girls. What fraction are boys?

A banjo has 5 strings. What fraction are 2 strings?

$\dfrac{2}{5}$

Name $\dfrac{3}{4}$ of the stringed instruments on this fun flap.

$\dfrac{1}{4}$ of the 4 kids in a family play banjo. How many don't play banjo?

$\dfrac{4}{10} = \dfrac{\square}{5}$

$\dfrac{6}{9} = \dfrac{\square}{3}$

$\dfrac{3}{4}$

$\dfrac{2}{8}$

harp

$\dfrac{\square}{3} = \dfrac{6}{12}$

$\dfrac{1}{4} = \dfrac{2}{\square}$

banjo

4 Egg-Xactly!

Rename the fractions in lowest terms.
Pick your favorite feathery friend to start.

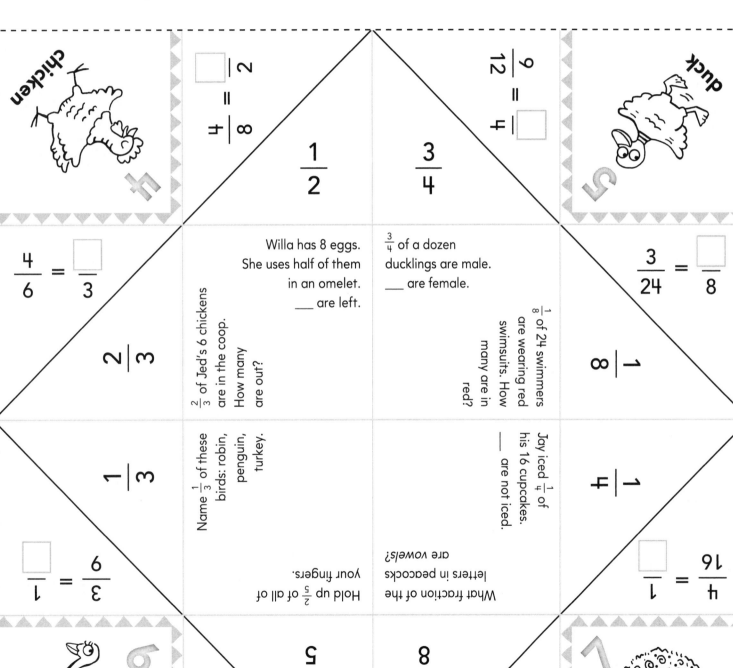

chicken

4

duck

5

$\dfrac{8}{4} = \dfrac{2}{\Box}$

$\dfrac{1}{2}$

$\dfrac{3}{4}$

$\dfrac{9}{12} = \dfrac{\Box}{4}$

$\dfrac{4}{6} = \dfrac{\Box}{3}$

Willa has 8 eggs. She uses half of them in an omelet. ___ are left.

$\dfrac{3}{4}$ of a dozen ducklings are male. ___ are female.

$\dfrac{3}{24} = \dfrac{\Box}{8}$

$\dfrac{2}{3}$

$\dfrac{2}{3}$ of Jed's 6 chickens are in the coop. How many are out?

$\dfrac{1}{8}$ of 24 swimmers are wearing red swimsuits. How many are in red?

$\dfrac{1}{8}$

$\dfrac{1}{3}$

Name $\dfrac{1}{3}$ of these birds: robin, penguin, turkey.

Jay iced $\dfrac{1}{4}$ of his 16 cupcakes. ___ are not iced.

$\dfrac{1}{4}$

$\dfrac{3}{6} = \dfrac{1}{\Box}$

Hold up $\dfrac{2}{5}$ of all of your fingers.

What fraction of the letters in peacocks are vowels?

$\dfrac{4}{16} = \dfrac{1}{\Box}$

ostrich

6

$\dfrac{2}{5}$

$\dfrac{3}{8}$

peacock

7

$\dfrac{4}{10} = \dfrac{2}{\Box}$

$\dfrac{6}{16} = \dfrac{3}{\Box}$

5 Bakery Bites

Which fraction is greater?
Pick your favorite bakery treat to start.

cake

3

$\dfrac{1}{4}$ or $\dfrac{1}{5}$

$\dfrac{1}{4}$

$\dfrac{3}{8}$

$\dfrac{1}{4}$ or $\dfrac{3}{8}$

cookies

4

$\dfrac{4}{6}$ or $\dfrac{3}{4}$

You might laugh in $\frac{1}{4}$ hour. $\frac{1}{4}$ hour is how many minutes?

Take 8 steps. Walk backward for $\frac{3}{8}$ of the steps.

$\dfrac{3}{6}$ or $\dfrac{1}{3}$

$\dfrac{3}{4}$

Name $\frac{3}{4}$ of the seasons.

Name another fraction that equals $\frac{3}{6}$.

$\dfrac{3}{6}$

$\dfrac{2}{4}$

Half of a 4-day trip was sunny. How many days were rainy?

$\frac{3}{5} = \frac{\square}{10}$ What number goes in the box?

$\dfrac{3}{5}$

$\dfrac{2}{2}$ or $\dfrac{84}{4}$

A pie is cut into 4 slices. How many slices make $\frac{1}{2}$ of the pie?

What fraction of the letters in *cupcakes* are consonants?

$\dfrac{2}{10}$ or $\dfrac{3}{5}$

pie

5

$\dfrac{1}{2}$ or $\dfrac{1}{3}$

$\dfrac{1}{2}$

$\dfrac{5}{8}$

$\dfrac{1}{4}$ or $\dfrac{5}{8}$

cupcakes

6

6 Up, Up, and Away

Which mixed number is greater?
Pick your favorite flying object to start.

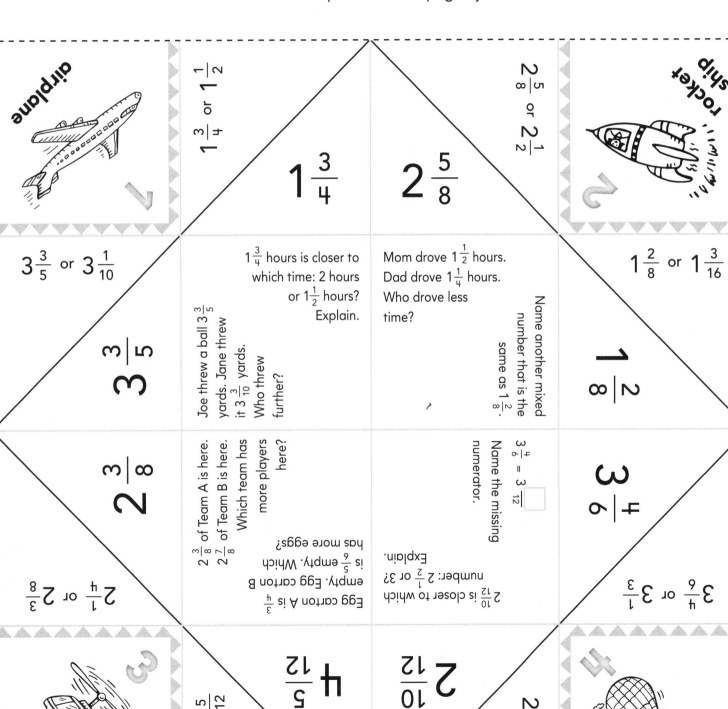

airplane
1

$1\frac{3}{4}$ or $1\frac{1}{2}$

$2\frac{5}{8}$ or $2\frac{1}{2}$

rocket ship
2

$1\frac{3}{4}$

$2\frac{5}{8}$

$3\frac{3}{5}$ or $3\frac{1}{10}$

$1\frac{3}{4}$ hours is closer to which time: 2 hours or $1\frac{1}{2}$ hours? Explain.

Mom drove $1\frac{1}{2}$ hours. Dad drove $1\frac{1}{4}$ hours. Who drove less time?

$1\frac{2}{8}$ or $1\frac{3}{16}$

$3\frac{3}{5}$

Joe threw a ball $3\frac{3}{5}$ yards. Jane threw it $3\frac{3}{10}$ yards. Who threw further?

Name another mixed number that is the same as $1\frac{2}{8}$.

$1\frac{2}{8}$

$2\frac{3}{8}$

$2\frac{3}{8}$ of Team A is here. $2\frac{7}{8}$ of Team B is here. Which team has more players here?

Egg carton A is $\frac{3}{4}$ empty. Egg carton B is $\frac{5}{6}$ empty. Which has more eggs?

$2\frac{10}{12}$ is closer to which number: $2\frac{1}{2}$ or 3? Explain.

$3\frac{4}{6} = 3\frac{\square}{12}$ Name the missing numerator.

$3\frac{4}{6}$

$2\frac{1}{4}$ or $2\frac{3}{8}$

$4\frac{5}{12}$

$2\frac{10}{12}$

$3\frac{4}{6}$ or $3\frac{1}{3}$

helicopter
3

$4\frac{1}{4}$ or $4\frac{5}{12}$

hot-air balloon
4

$2\frac{2}{3}$ or $2\frac{10}{12}$

7 Brrr!

Which mixed number is larger?
Pick your favorite winter board sport to start.

sledding

5

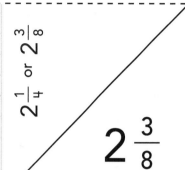

$2\frac{1}{4}$ or $2\frac{3}{8}$

$1\frac{3}{10}$ or $1\frac{1}{5}$

skiing

6

$2\frac{3}{8}$

$1\frac{3}{10}$

$3\frac{2}{3}$ or $3\frac{1}{6}$

$2\frac{3}{8}$ is closer to which number: 2 or $2\frac{1}{2}$? Explain.

10 hats in each row. How many hats in $\frac{2}{10}$ rows?

$2\frac{5}{8}$ or $2\frac{5}{16}$

$3\frac{2}{3}$

Name the missing numerator.
$3\frac{2}{3} = 3\frac{\square}{6}$

Name the missing denominator.
$2\frac{4}{8} = 2\frac{1}{\square}$

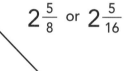

$2\frac{5}{8}$

$3\frac{7}{10}$

10 books per box. $3\frac{7}{10}$ boxes plus ____ books makes 4 boxes.

Which time is longer: $1\frac{3}{4}$ hours or 1 hour 30 minutes?

$1\frac{3}{4}$

$3\frac{1}{2}$ or $3\frac{7}{10}$

12 inches = 1 foot. How many inches in $2\frac{1}{2}$ feet?

Is $4\frac{1}{8}$ closer to 4 or $4\frac{1}{2}$? Explain.

$1\frac{3}{4}$ or $1\frac{1}{3}$

ice skating

7

$2\frac{5}{12}$ or $2\frac{1}{2}$

$2\frac{1}{2}$

$4\frac{3}{16}$

$4\frac{1}{8}$ or $4\frac{3}{16}$

snowboarding

8

8 Fruity Flavors

Rename each improper fraction as a whole number.
Pick your favorite fruit to start.

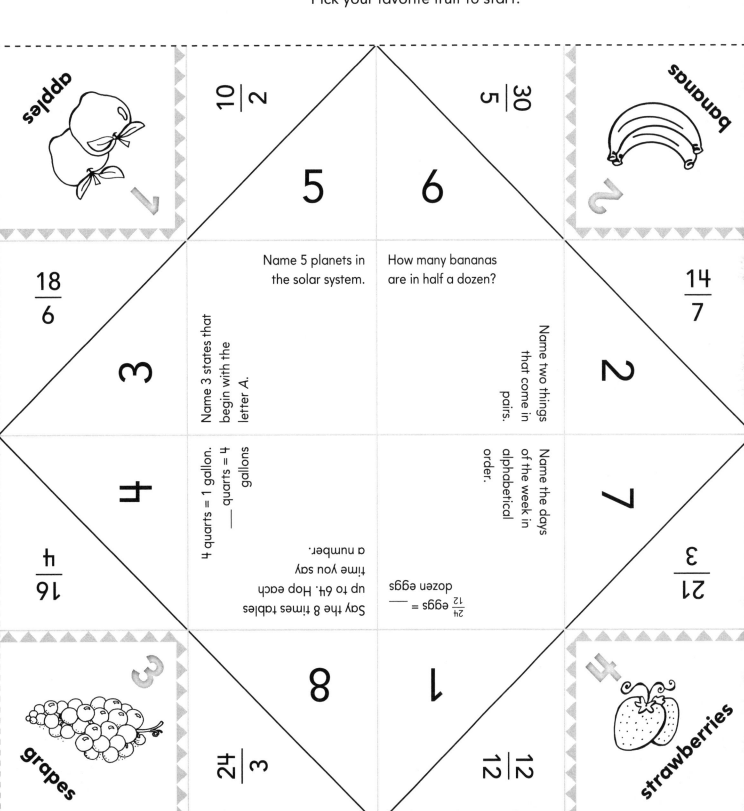

apples

$\frac{10}{2}$

5

6

$\frac{30}{5}$

bananas

$\frac{18}{6}$

3

Name 5 planets in the solar system.

How many bananas are in half a dozen?

2

$\frac{14}{7}$

Name 3 states that begin with the letter A.

Name two things that come in pairs.

$\frac{16}{4}$

4

4 quarts = 1 gallon.
___ quarts = 4 gallons

Name the days of the week in alphabetical order.

7

$\frac{21}{3}$

Say the 8 times tables up to 64. Hop each time you say a number.

$\frac{24}{12}$ eggs = ___ dozen eggs

grapes

$\frac{24}{3}$

8

1

$\frac{12}{12}$

strawberries

9 Book It!

Rename each improper fraction as a mixed number.
Pick your favorite genre to start.

 science fiction 5

$\frac{4}{10}$

$2\frac{2}{4}$

$2\frac{2}{9}$

$\frac{20}{9}$

mystery 6

$\frac{11}{6}$

$1\frac{5}{6}$

$2\frac{2}{4} = 2\frac{\square}{2}$
Name the missing numerator.

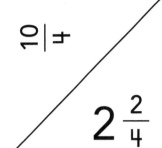

$2\frac{2}{9} = 2\frac{4}{\square}$
Name the missing denominator.

You've read $\frac{1}{2}$ of a 36-page book. How many pages have you read?

$4\frac{1}{3}$

$\frac{13}{3}$

$1\frac{5}{6} + \frac{\square}{6} = 2$
Name the missing numerator.

$7\frac{1}{2}$

How many pies are needed to give 20 people $\frac{1}{2}$ a pie each?

Which is greater: $2\frac{3}{7}$ or $2\frac{1}{2}$?

$2\frac{3}{7}$

$\frac{17}{7}$

$\frac{15}{2}$

Which is greater: $1\frac{3}{5}$ or $1\frac{1}{2}$?

$2\frac{4}{8} = 2\frac{1}{\square}$
Name the missing denominator.

$1\frac{3}{5}$

$2\frac{4}{8}$

 fantasy 7

$\frac{8}{5}$

$\frac{20}{8}$

nonfiction 8

10 Looking Up

Rename each mixed number as an improper fraction.
Pick your favorite object in the sky to start.

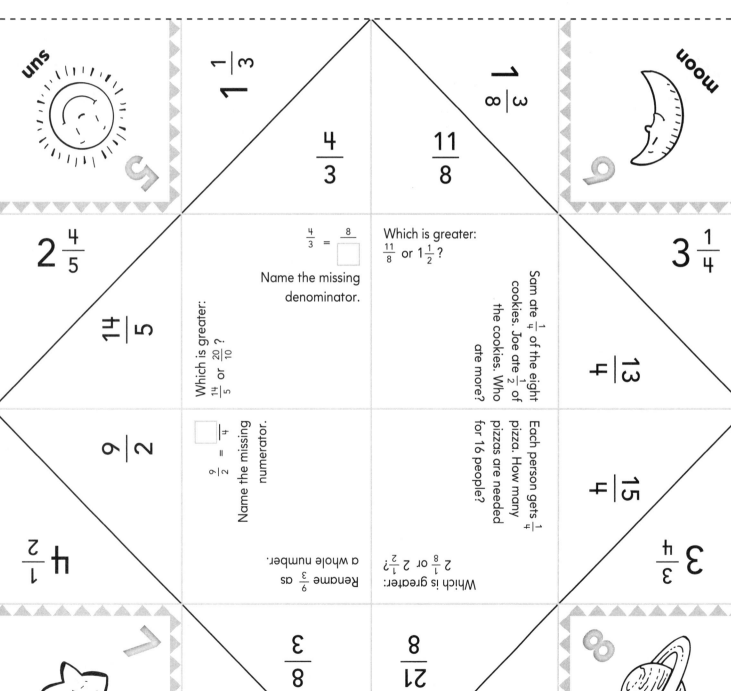

sun 5

$1\frac{1}{3}$

$\frac{4}{3}$

$1\frac{3}{8}$

$\frac{11}{8}$

moon 6

$2\frac{4}{5}$

$\frac{14}{5}$

$\frac{4}{3} = \frac{8}{\Box}$

Name the missing denominator.

Which is greater: $\frac{11}{8}$ or $1\frac{1}{2}$?

Sam ate $\frac{1}{4}$ of the eight cookies. Joe ate $\frac{1}{2}$ of the cookies. Who ate more?

$3\frac{1}{4}$

Which is greater: $\frac{14}{5}$ or $\frac{20}{10}$?

$\frac{9}{2}$

$\frac{\Box}{4} = \frac{9}{2}$

Name the missing numerator.

Each person gets $\frac{1}{4}$ of pizza. How many pizzas are needed for 16 people?

$\frac{13}{4}$

$4\frac{1}{2}$

Rename $\frac{9}{3}$ as a whole number.

Which is greater: $2\frac{1}{8}$ or $2\frac{1}{2}$?

$\frac{15}{4}$

$3\frac{3}{4}$

star 7

$\frac{3}{8}$

$\frac{21}{8}$

Saturn 8

$2\frac{2}{3}$

$2\frac{5}{8}$

11 Spring Flowers

Add the fractions.
Pick your favorite flower to start.

rose · 3

$$\frac{1}{3} + \frac{1}{3}$$

$$\frac{2}{3}$$

$$\frac{4}{5}$$

$$\frac{3}{5} + \frac{1}{5}$$

tulip · 4

$$\frac{1}{4} + \frac{2}{4}$$

Which is greater:
$\frac{2}{3}$ or $\frac{1}{2}$?

$\frac{4}{5}$ of the flowers
are yellow. What
fraction is not
yellow?

$$\frac{4}{10} + \frac{5}{10}$$

$$\frac{3}{4}$$

Name the missing
numerator.

$$\frac{2}{4} = \frac{\Box}{2}$$

Hold up $\frac{9}{10}$ of
your fingers.

$$\frac{9}{10}$$

$$\frac{5}{7}$$

It rained $\frac{5}{7}$ of the
week. How many
days were dry?

Name the missing
numerator.

$$\frac{7}{8} + \frac{\Box}{8} = 1$$

Name the missing
denominator.

$$\frac{6}{9} = \frac{2}{\Box}$$

Rename $\frac{4}{6}$
as thirds.

$$\frac{4}{6}$$

$$\frac{2}{7} + \frac{3}{7}$$

$$\frac{7}{8}$$

$$\frac{6}{9}$$

$$\frac{1}{6} + \frac{3}{6}$$

daffodil · 5

$$\frac{3}{8} + \frac{4}{8}$$

$$\frac{4}{9} + \frac{2}{9}$$

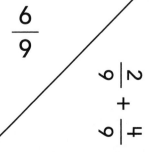

daisy · 6

12 It's Only Myth Believe

Subtract the fractions.
Pick your favorite mythical character to start.

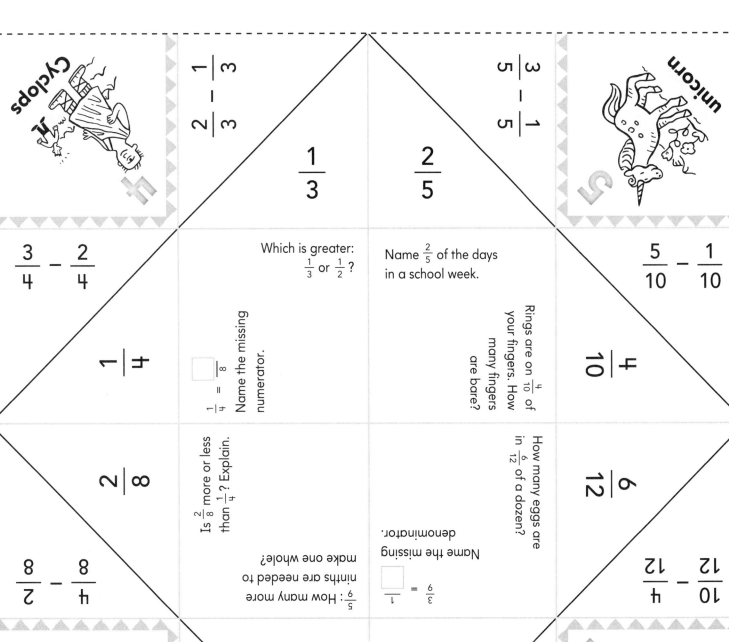

Cyclops
4

$\frac{2}{3} - \frac{1}{3}$

$\frac{1}{3}$

Which is greater: $\frac{1}{3}$ or $\frac{1}{2}$?

$\frac{3}{4} - \frac{2}{4}$

$\frac{1}{4}$

Name the missing numerator.

$\frac{1}{4} = \frac{\boxed{}}{8}$

$\frac{2}{8}$

Is $\frac{2}{8}$ more or less than $\frac{1}{4}$? Explain.

$\frac{4}{8} - \frac{2}{8}$

$\frac{5}{9}$: How many more ninths are needed to make one whole?

$\frac{5}{9}$

$\frac{6}{9} - \frac{3}{9}$

$\frac{3}{5} - \frac{1}{5}$

$\frac{2}{5}$

Name $\frac{2}{5}$ of the days in a school week.

Rings are on $\frac{4}{10}$ of your fingers. How many fingers are bare?

$\frac{4}{10}$

$\frac{6}{12}$

How many eggs are in $\frac{6}{12}$ of a dozen?

Name the missing denominator.

$\frac{3}{9} = \frac{1}{\boxed{}}$

$\frac{3}{6}$

$\frac{5}{6} - \frac{2}{6}$

unicorn
5

$\frac{5}{10} - \frac{1}{10}$

$\frac{10}{12} - \frac{4}{12}$

Sphinx
7

Pegasus
6

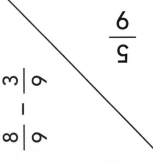

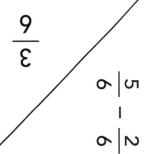

Skill > Adding Mixed Numbers

13 Play Ball!

Add the mixed numbers.
Pick your favorite ball game to start.

basketball **2**

$1\frac{1}{4} + 2\frac{1}{4}$

$3\frac{2}{4}$

$4\frac{4}{5}$

$3\frac{1}{5} + 1\frac{3}{5}$

soccer **3**

$2\frac{2}{8} + 3\frac{3}{8}$

How many halves are in $3\frac{2}{4}$?

5 gloves in each box. How many gloves in $4\frac{4}{5}$ boxes?

$2\frac{2}{6} + 4\frac{3}{6}$

$5\frac{5}{8}$

$5\frac{5}{8}$: How many more eighths are needed to make six wholes?

Name the missing numerator.

$6\frac{5}{6} = 6\frac{\Box}{12}$

$6\frac{5}{6}$

$8\frac{4}{7}$

How many days are in $8\frac{4}{7}$ weeks?

Name the missing denominator.

$13\frac{3}{4} = 13\frac{6}{\Box}$

$13\frac{3}{4}$

$4\frac{3}{7} + 4\frac{1}{7}$

Which is greater: $14\frac{2}{3}$ or $14\frac{1}{2}$?

9 golf balls per box. $3\frac{7}{9}$ boxes plus ___ balls makes 4 full boxes.

$7\frac{1}{4} + 6\frac{2}{4}$

tennis **4**

$10\frac{1}{3} + 4\frac{1}{3}$

$14\frac{2}{3}$

$11\frac{5}{9}$

$5\frac{2}{9} + 6\frac{3}{9}$

golf **5**

14 Creepy Crawlies

Subtract the mixed numbers.
Pick your favorite bug to start.

ant

2

$2\frac{3}{4} - 1\frac{1}{4}$

$1\frac{2}{4}$

$2\frac{3}{8}$

$6\frac{5}{8} - 4\frac{2}{8}$

spider

3

$5\frac{2}{3} - 1\frac{1}{3}$

$1\frac{2}{4} = 1\frac{1}{\boxed{}}$

Name the missing denominator.

Rename $2\frac{3}{8}$ as an improper fraction.

$8\frac{5}{6} - 2\frac{1}{6}$

$4\frac{1}{3}$

Which is greater: $4\frac{2}{3}$ or $4\frac{1}{2}$?

Rename $6\frac{4}{6}$ in its lowest term.

$6\frac{4}{6}$

$5\frac{1}{4}$

Rename $5\frac{1}{4}$ as an improper fraction.

Rename $8\frac{3}{9}$ in its lowest term.

$8\frac{3}{9}$

$7\frac{3}{4} - 2\frac{2}{4}$

Rename $7\frac{5}{10}$ in its lowest term.

Which is greater: $3\frac{1}{2}$ or $7\frac{2}{7}$? Explain.

$10\frac{7}{9} - 2\frac{4}{9}$

caterpillar

4

$12\frac{7}{10} - 5\frac{2}{10}$

$7\frac{5}{10}$

$3\frac{2}{5}$

$4\frac{4}{5} - 1\frac{2}{5}$

ladybug

5

15 Top It Off

Add or subtract the mixed numbers.
Pick your favorite hat to start.

baseball cap

4

$5\frac{2}{5} + 1\frac{1}{5}$

$6\frac{3}{5}$

$9\frac{8}{12}$

$12\frac{11}{12} - 3\frac{3}{12}$

top hat

5

$2\frac{1}{4} + 5\frac{1}{4}$

Is $6\frac{3}{5}$ more or less than half a dozen? Explain.

$9\frac{8}{12} + \boxed{} = 10$
What number goes in the box?

$10\frac{6}{7} - 7\frac{1}{7}$

$7\frac{2}{4}$

Which is greater: $7\frac{2}{4}$ or $7\frac{1}{2}$? Explain.

$3\frac{5}{7} + \boxed{} = 4$
What number goes in the box?

$3\frac{5}{7}$

$8\frac{7}{8}$

How many more eighths make 9 wholes?

Which is greater: $5\frac{1}{9}$ or $5\frac{3}{3}$? Explain.

$5\frac{1}{9}$

$6\frac{5}{8} + 2\frac{2}{8}$

Rename $4\frac{5}{10}$ in lowest terms.

Rename $1\frac{4}{6}$ in lowest terms.

$8\frac{3}{9} - 3\frac{2}{9}$

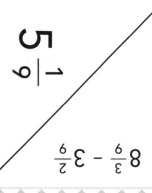

fedora

6

$2\frac{5}{6} - 1\frac{1}{6}$

$1\frac{4}{6}$

$4\frac{5}{10}$

$1\frac{2}{10} + 3\frac{3}{10}$

beret

7

16 Get on Board!

Rename the fractions as decimals to the tenths place.
Pick your favorite board rider to start.

surfer
5

kiteboarder
6

$\frac{5}{10} = $. ____

.3   .5

$\frac{3}{10} = $. ____

$\frac{7}{10} = $. ____

$\frac{4}{10}$ of the kids walk to school. Rename this fraction as a decimal.

Rename .5 as a fraction in its lowest term.

$\frac{1}{10} = $. ____

.7

9 out of 10 test items are correct. What decimal is that?

What end punctuation does a decimal point look like?

.1

.2

Dad fried 3 out of 10 eggs. What decimal is that?

$\frac{2}{10}$ of your fingers are thumbs. Rename this fraction as a decimal.

Sam ate $\frac{1}{10}$ of a pie. Use a decimal to tell how much pie is left.

.6 players on the team are boys. Rename the decimal as a fraction.

.4

$\frac{2}{10} = $. ____

$\frac{4}{10} = $. ____

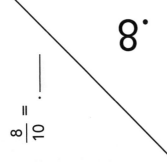
skateboarder
7

8.   9.

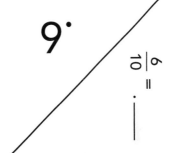

snowboarder
8

$\frac{8}{10} = $. ____

$\frac{6}{10} = $. ____

17 Dog Days

Rename the fractions as decimals to the hundredths place.
Pick your favorite dog to start.

St. Bernard 3

$\frac{5}{100}$ = . ____

$\frac{2}{100}$ = . ____

.05

.08

You got 5 out of 100 answers wrong. What decimal is that?

8 out of 100 kids have freckles. What decimal is that?

$\frac{8}{100}$ = . ____

Poodle 4

$\frac{4}{100}$ = . ____

.02

2 out of 100 kids don't have pets. What decimal is that?

You missed 4 out of 100 school days. What decimal is that?

.04

.03

3 out of 100 eggs are cracked. What decimal is that?

It rained 6 out of 100 days. What decimal is that?

.06

$\frac{3}{100}$ = . ____

1 out of 100 families live on farms. What decimal is that?

7 out of 100 apples have worms. What decimal is that?

$\frac{6}{100}$ = . ____

Chihuahua 5

$\frac{1}{100}$ = . ____

.01

.07

$\frac{7}{100}$ = . ____

Dalmatian 6

18 Indoor Sports

Rename the mixed numbers as decimals to the tenths place.
Pick your favorite indoor sport to start.

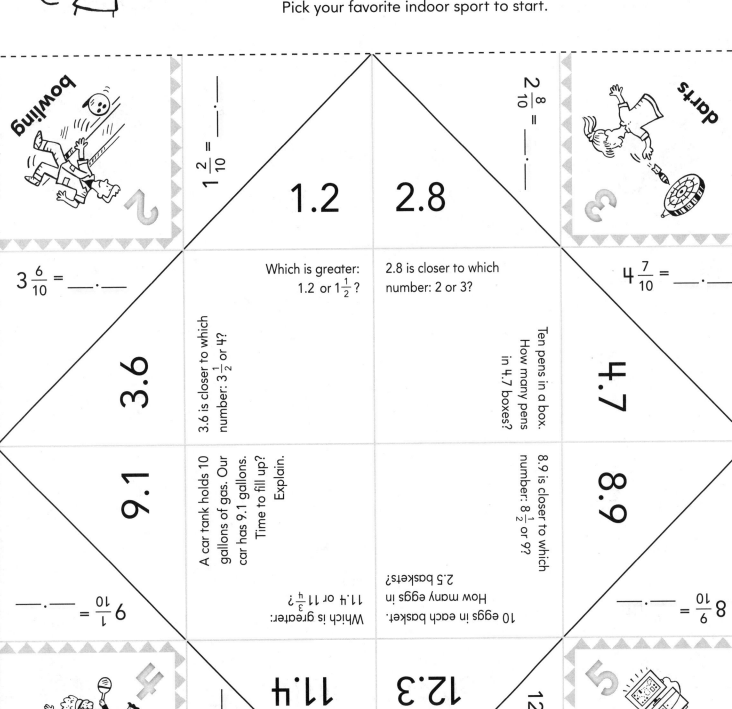

bowling

2

$1\frac{2}{10} =$ ___ . ___

$2\frac{8}{10} =$ ___ . ___

darts

3

1.2

2.8

$3\frac{6}{10} =$ ___ . ___

Which is greater:
1.2 or $1\frac{1}{2}$?

2.8 is closer to which
number: 2 or 3?

$4\frac{7}{10} =$ ___ . ___

3.6

3.6 is closer to which
number: $3\frac{1}{2}$ or 4?

Ten pens in a box.
How many pens
in 4.7 boxes?

4.7

9.1

A car tank holds 10
gallons of gas. Our
car has 9.1 gallons.
Time to fill up?
Explain.

8.9 is closer to which
number: $8\frac{1}{2}$ or 9?

8.9

$9\frac{1}{10} =$ ___ . ___

Which is greater:
11.4 or $11\frac{3}{4}$?

10 eggs in each basket.
How many eggs in
2.5 baskets?

$8\frac{6}{10} =$ ___ . ___

ping pong

4

$11\frac{4}{10} =$ ___ . ___

11.4

12.3

$12\frac{3}{10} =$ ___ . ___

video game

5

19 Black and White

Rename the mixed numbers as decimals to the hundredths place.
Pick your favorite black and white animal to start.

penguin

4

$2\frac{8}{100} =$ ——.——

2.08

3.05

$3\frac{5}{100} =$ ——.——

panda

5

$1\frac{3}{100} =$ ——.——

2.08 is closer to which number: 2 or 3?

3.05 is closer to which number: 3 or $3\frac{1}{2}$?

$4\frac{6}{100} =$ ——.——

1.03

Which is greater: 1.03 or 1.30?

How many pennies in $4.06?

4.06

10.09

Is 10.09 more or less than 10? Explain.

Which equals $9.07: 907 pennies or 970 pennies?

9.07

$10\frac{9}{100} =$ ——.——

Is 12.06 inches more or less than one foot?

Which is more: $8.04 or 804 pennies? Explain.

$9\frac{7}{100} =$ ——.——

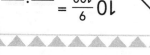

zebra

6

12.06

8.04

$8\frac{4}{100} =$ ——.——

$12\frac{6}{100} =$ ——.——

skunk

7

20 Awesome Outings

Compare the decimals. Which is greater?
Pick your favorite outdoor activity to start.

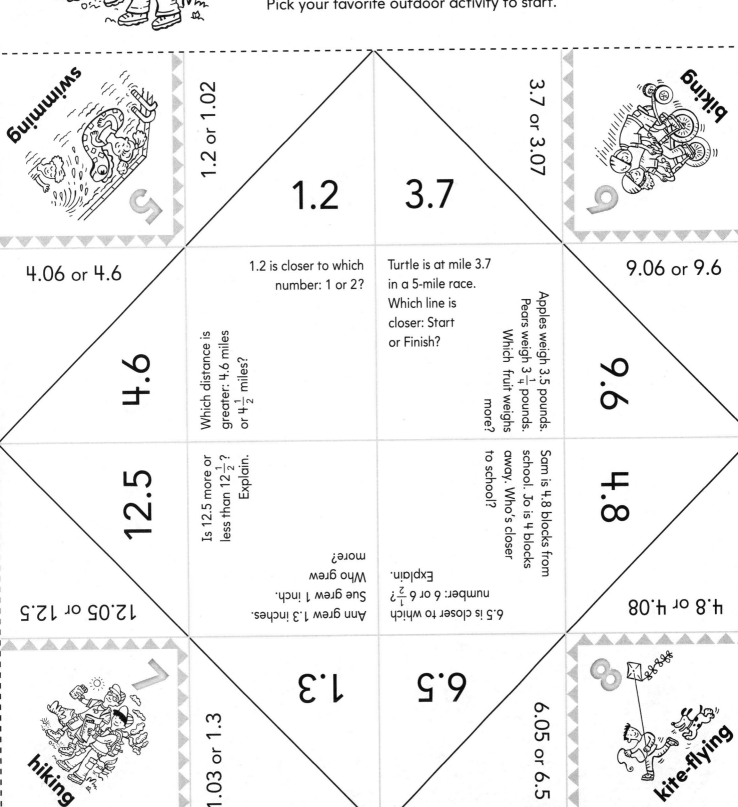

swimming

5

1.2 or 1.02

3.7 or 3.07

biking

6

1.2

3.7

4.06 or 4.6

1.2 is closer to which number: 1 or 2?

Turtle is at mile 3.7 in a 5-mile race. Which line is closer: Start or Finish?

9.06 or 9.6

4.6

Which distance is greater: 4.6 miles or 4½ miles?

Apples weigh 3.5 pounds. Pears weigh 3¼ pounds. Which fruit weighs more?

9.6

12.5

Is 12.5 more or less than 12½? Explain.

Sam is 4.8 blocks from school. Jo is 4 blocks away. Who's closer to school?

4.8

12.05 or 12.5

Ann grew 1.3 inches. Sue grew 1 inch. Who grew more?

6.5 is closer to which number: 6 or 6½? Explain.

4.8 or 4.08

hiking

7

1.03 or 1.3

1.3

6.5

6.05 or 6.5

kite-flying

8

21 Time With Friends

Add.
Pick your favorite way to spend time with friends to start.

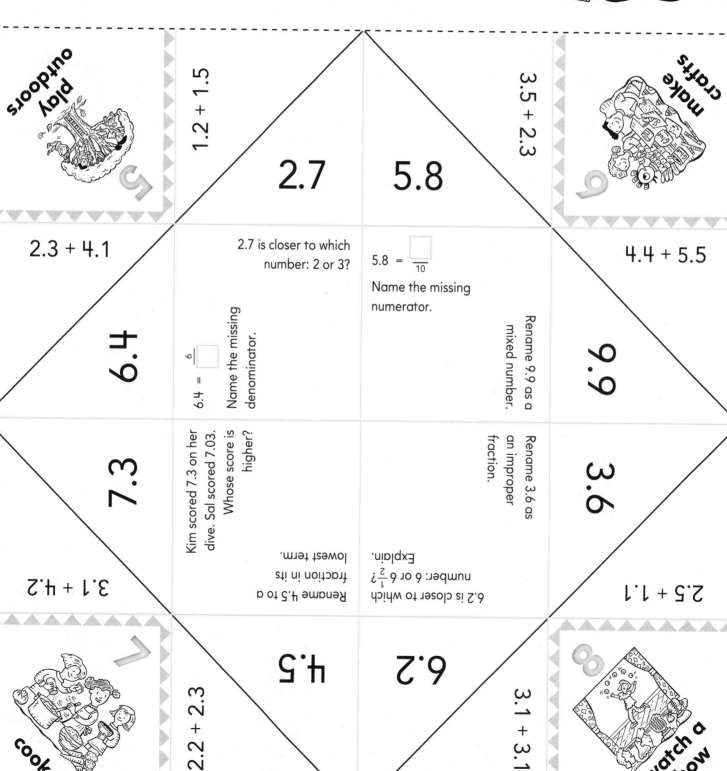

play outdoors

1.2 + 1.5

2.7

5.8

3.5 + 2.3

make crafts

2.3 + 4.1

2.7 is closer to which number: 2 or 3?

$5.8 = \dfrac{\boxed{}}{10}$
Name the missing numerator.

4.4 + 5.5

6.4

$6.4 = \dfrac{6}{\boxed{}}$
Name the missing denominator.

Rename 9.9 as a mixed number.

9.9

7.3

Kim scored 7.3 on her dive. Sal scored 7.03. Whose score is higher?

Rename 4.5 to a fraction in its lowest term.

6.2 is closer to which number: 6 or $6\frac{1}{2}$? Explain.

Rename 3.6 as an improper fraction.

3.6

3.1 + 4.2

2.5 + 1.1

cook

2.2 + 2.3

4.5

6.2

3.1 + 3.1

watch a show

22 Sea Scene

Add.
Pick your favorite sea creature to start.

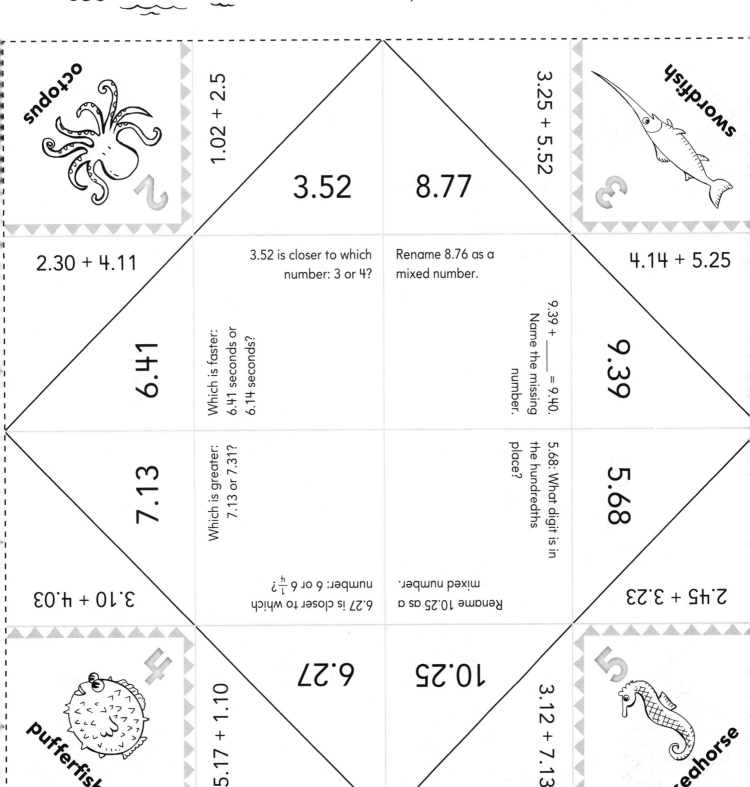

octopus

2

swordfish

3

1.02 + 2.5

3.52

8.77

3.25 + 5.52

2.30 + 4.11

3.52 is closer to which number: 3 or 4?

Rename 8.76 as a mixed number.

4.14 + 5.25

6.41

Which is faster: 6.41 seconds or 6.14 seconds?

9.39 + _____ = 9.40. Name the missing number.

9.39

7.13

Which is greater: 7.13 or 7.31?

5.68: What digit is in the hundredths place?

5.68

3.10 + 4.03

6.27 is closer to which number: 6 or 6 1/4?

Rename 10.25 as a mixed number.

2.45 + 3.23

5.17 + 1.10

6.27

10.25

3.12 + 7.13

pufferfish

4

seahorse

5

23 Cats Can

Add.
Pick your favorite wild cat to start.

leopard

$1.25 + $1.20

$2.45

$4.99

$3.89 + $1.10

lion

$2.10 + $3.08

Which amount is greater: $2.45 or $2.50?

One penny is what fraction of a dollar?

$4.40 + $5.47

$5.18

Add $\frac{1}{4}$ dollar to $5.00. How much is that?

You had $2.23. You earned 1\frac{1}{2}$ dollars. How much do you have now?

$9.87

$3.54

Rename $3.50 as an improper fraction: ____ dollars

A shirt costs $4.51. You pay 4$\frac{3}{4}$ dollars. What is your change?

$4.61

$1.52 + $2.02

Which amount is greater: $5.76 or a five-dollar bill and 3 quarters?

Which would you rather have: $5.20 or a five-dollar bill and 2 dimes? Explain.

$2.31 + $2.30

tiger

$4.23 + $1.53

$5.76

$8.20

$5.10 + $3.10

lynx

24 Just Relax

Subtract.
Pick your favorite way to relax to start.

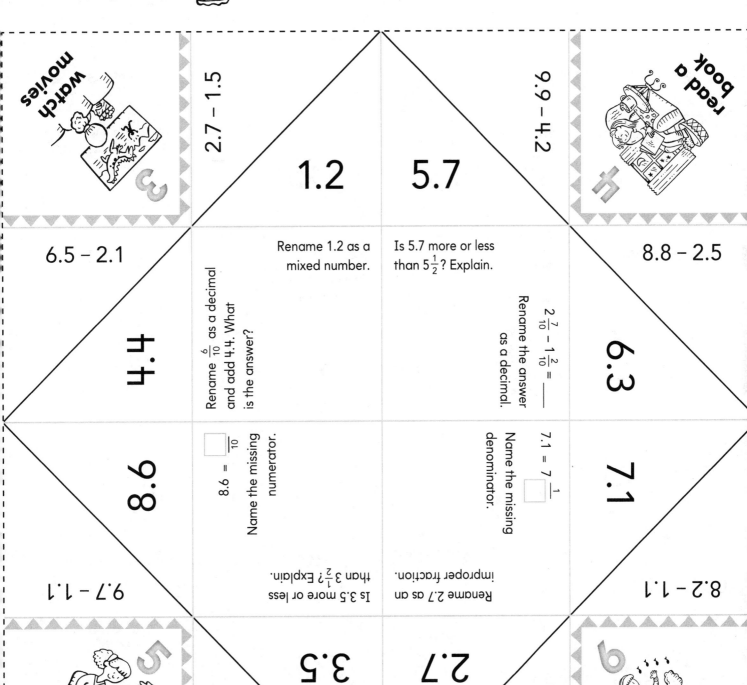

watch movies 3

2.7 – 1.5

1.2

5.7

9.9 – 4.2

read a book 4

6.5 – 2.1

Rename 1.2 as a mixed number.

Is 5.7 more or less than $5\frac{1}{2}$? Explain.

8.8 – 2.5

4.4

Rename $\frac{6}{10}$ as a decimal and add 4.4. What is the answer?

$2\frac{7}{10} - 1\frac{2}{10} =$
Rename the answer as a decimal.

6.3

8.6

$8.6 = \frac{\square}{10}$
Name the missing numerator.

$7.1 = 7\frac{1}{\square}$
Name the missing denominator.

7.1

9.7 – 1.1

Is 3.5 more or less than $3\frac{1}{2}$? Explain.

Rename 2.7 as an improper fraction.

8.2 – 1.1

play games 5

5.7 – 2.2

3.5

2.7

3.9 – 1.2

listen to music 6

25 Art Attack!

Subtract.
Pick your favorite art form to start.

painting

6.54 – 2.21

4.33

3.20

7.31 – 4.11

sculpture

2.96 – 1.50

Rename 4.33 as a mixed number.

$3 \frac{45}{100} - 1 \frac{13}{100} =$ _____
Rename the answer as a decimal.

6.52 – 1.51

1.46

Rename $\frac{4}{100}$ as a decimal and add 4.46. What is the answer?

Which is faster: 5.01 seconds or 5.10 seconds?

5.01

6.05

$6.05 = 6 \frac{\square}{100}$

Name the missing numerator.

Rename 4.07 as a mixed number.

4.07

9.25 – 3.20

Name the missing denominator.

$7.13 = 7 \frac{13}{\square}$

Rename 2.50 as a mixed number in its lowest term.

5.17 – 1.10

photography

9.16 – 4.03

5.13

2.22

3.45 – 1.23

computer graphics

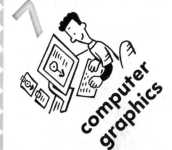

26 Shells to Go

Subtract.

Pick your favorite shell animal to start.

snail

5

$2.50 − $1.00

$1.50

$5.73

$9.96 − $4.23

turtle

6

$6.59 − $2.11

$1.50 = 1 □/100 dollars

Name the missing numerator.

$5.73 = 5 □⁻⁷³ dollars

Name the missing denominator.

$8.18 − $2.14

$4.48

Which amount is greater: $4.48 or 4 ½ dollars?

Subtract ¼ dollar from $6.36. How much is that?

$6.04

$4.30

9 35/100 dollars =

$ ___ . ___

A ball costs $3.01. You pay 3 ¼ dollars. What is your change?

A book costs $7.15. You pay $8.00. What is your change?

Which amount is greater: $2.82 or 2 ¾ dollars?

$7.15

$9.35 − $5.05

$3.01

$2.82

$8.25 − $1.10

crab

7

$5.27 − $2.26

$3.99 − $1.17

lobster

8

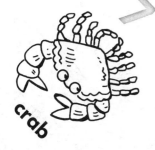

27 Desert Life

Name the shaded part of the shapes as fractions and percentages.
Pick your favorite desert animal to start.

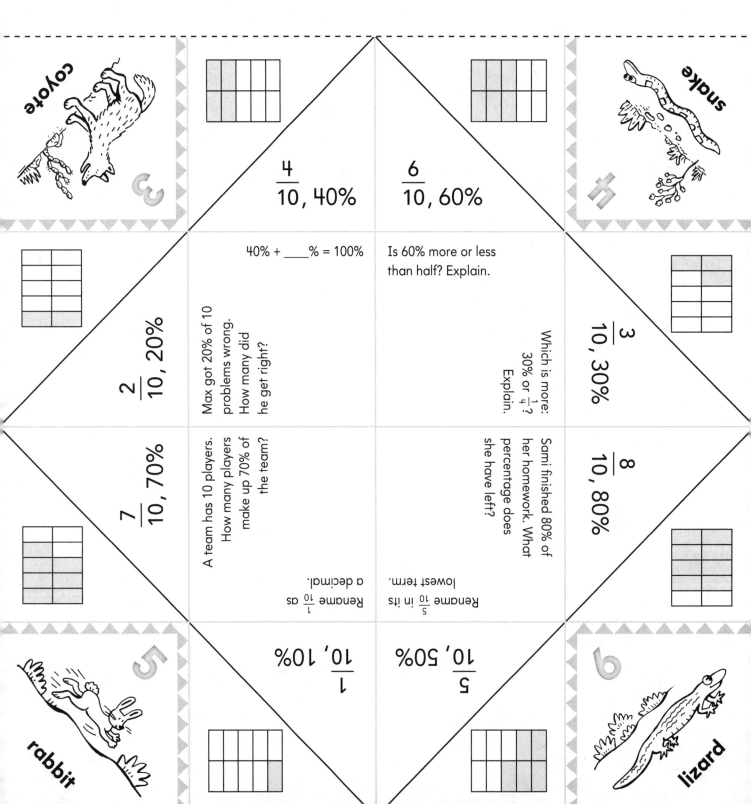

coyote 3

snake 4

$\frac{4}{10}, 40\%$

$\frac{6}{10}, 60\%$

40% + ____% = 100%

Is 60% more or less than half? Explain.

$\frac{2}{10}, 20\%$

Max got 20% of 10 problems wrong. How many did he get right?

Which is more: 30% or $\frac{1}{4}$? Explain.

$\frac{3}{10}, 30\%$

$\frac{7}{10}, 70\%$

A team has 10 players. How many players make up 70% of the team?

Sami finished 80% of her homework. What percentage does she have left?

$\frac{8}{10}, 80\%$

Rename $\frac{5}{10}$ in its lowest term.

Rename $\frac{1}{10}$ as a decimal.

rabbit 5

$\frac{1}{10}, 10\%$

$\frac{5}{10}, 50\%$

lizard 6

28 Whee!

Name the shaded part of the shapes as fractions in their lowest terms. Then name them as percentages. Pick your favorite ride to start.

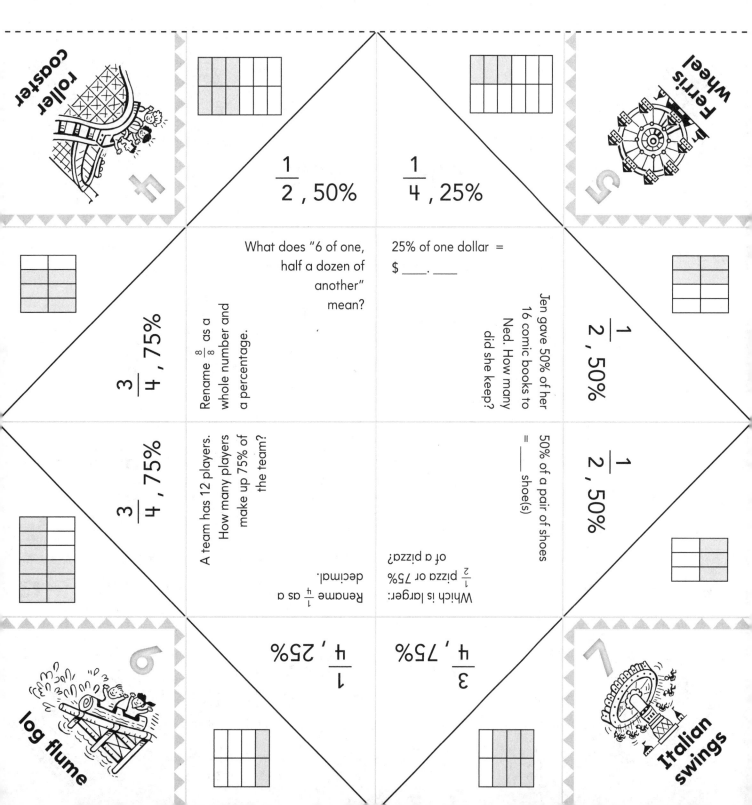

roller coaster

Ferris wheel

$\frac{1}{2}$, 50%

$\frac{1}{4}$, 25%

What does "6 of one, half a dozen of another" mean?

25% of one dollar = $ ___ . ___

Rename $\frac{8}{8}$ as a whole number and a percentage.

Jen gave 50% of her 16 comic books to Ned. How many did she keep?

$\frac{3}{4}$, 75%

$\frac{1}{2}$, 50%

$\frac{3}{4}$, 75%

A team has 12 players. How many players make up 75% of the team?

50% of a pair of shoes = ___ shoe(s)

$\frac{1}{2}$, 50%

Which is larger: $\frac{1}{2}$ pizza or 75% of a pizza?

Rename $\frac{1}{4}$ as a decimal.

$\frac{1}{4}$, 25%

$\frac{3}{4}$, 75%

log flume

Italian swings

29 Super Seasons

Rename the decimals as percentages.
Pick your favorite season to start.

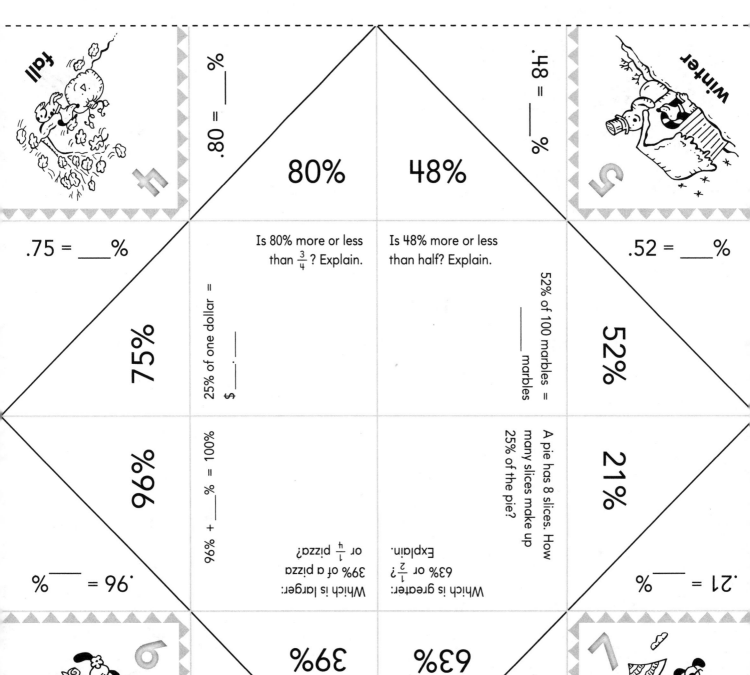

fall

4

$.80 =$ _____ %

80%

.48 = _____ %

48%

Winter

5

$.75 =$ _____ %

Is 80% more or less than $\frac{3}{4}$? Explain.

Is 48% more or less than half? Explain.

$.52 =$ _____ %

75%

25% of one dollar = $. _____

52% of 100 marbles = _____ marbles

52%

96%

96% + _____ % = 100%

A pie has 8 slices. How many slices make up 25% of the pie?

21%

$.96 =$ _____ %

Which is larger: 39% of a pizza or $\frac{1}{4}$ pizza?

Which is greater: 63% or $\frac{1}{2}$? Explain.

$.21 =$ _____ %

spring

6

$.39 =$ _____ %

39%

63%

.63 = _____ %

summer

7

30 Let's Go Shopping

What is the new price?
Pick your favorite store to start.

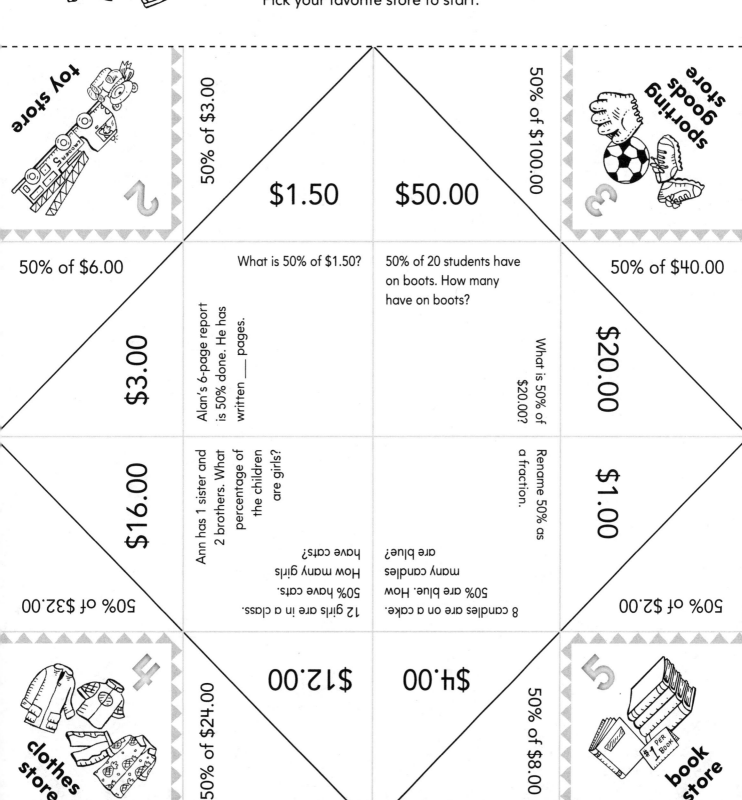

toy store 2

50% of $3.00

$1.50

$50.00

50% of $100.00

sporting goods store 3

50% of $6.00

What is 50% of $1.50?

50% of 20 students have on boots. How many have on boots?

50% of $40.00

$3.00

Alan's 6-page report is 50% done. He has written ____ pages.

What is 50% of $20.00?

$20.00

$16.00

Ann has 1 sister and 2 brothers. What percentage of the children are girls?

Rename 50% as a fraction.

$1.00

50% of $32.00

12 girls are in a class. 50% have cats. How many girls have cats?

8 candles are on a cake. 50% are blue. How many candles are blue?

50% of $2.00

clothes store 4

50% of $24.00

$12.00

$4.00

50% of $8.00

book store 5

31 Don't Rock the Boat!

What is the new price?

Pick your favorite boat to start.

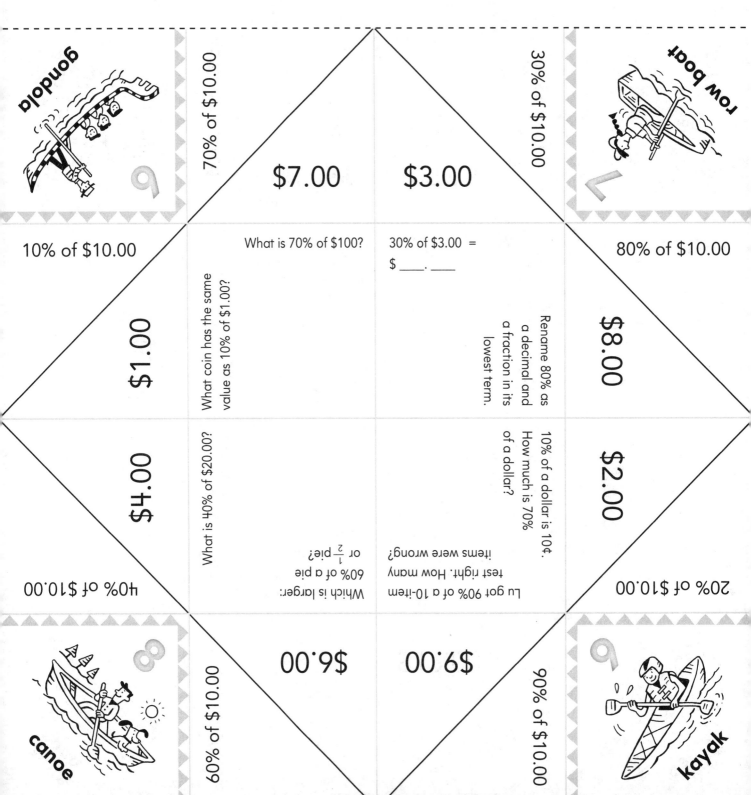

gondola

70% of $10.00

$7.00

$3.00

30% of $10.00

row boat

10% of $10.00

What is 70% of $100?

30% of $3.00 =

$ ____ . ____

80% of $10.00

$1.00

What coin has the same value as 10% of $1.00?

Rename 80% as a decimal and a fraction in its lowest term.

$8.00

$4.00

What is 40% of $20.00?

10% of a dollar is 10¢. How much is 70% of a dollar?

$2.00

40% of $10.00

Which is larger: 60% of a pie or $\frac{1}{2}$ pie?

Lu got 90% of a 10-item test right. How many items were wrong?

20% of $10.00

canoe

60% of $10.00

$6.00

$6.00

90% of $10.00

kayak

32 Fantastic Fair Food

What is the new price?
Pick your favorite fair food to start.

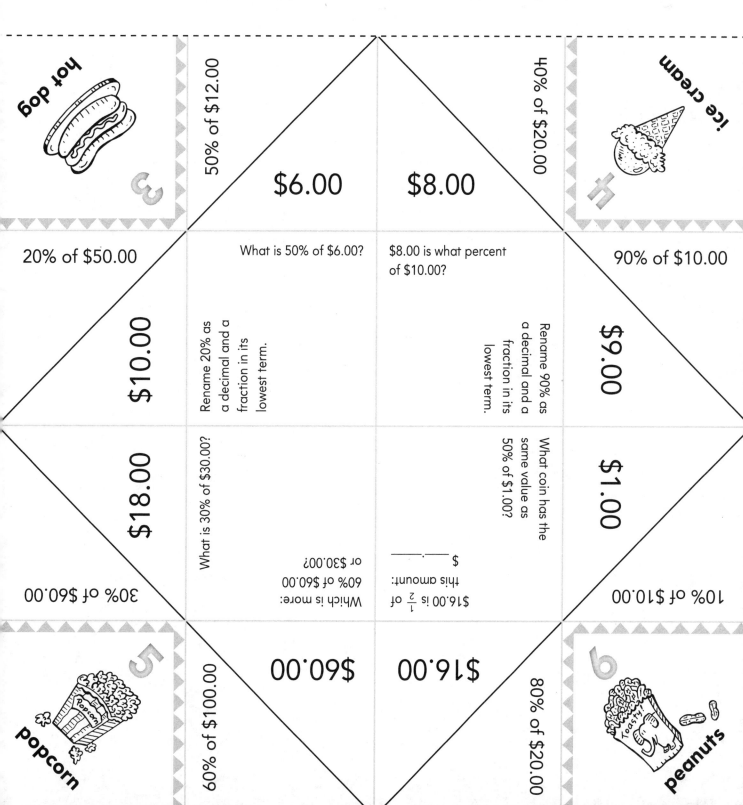

hot dog

3

50% of $12.00

$6.00

$8.00

40% of $20.00

ice cream

4

20% of $50.00

What is 50% of $6.00?

$8.00 is what percent of $10.00?

90% of $10.00

$10.00

Rename 20% as a decimal and a fraction in its lowest term.

Rename 90% as a decimal and a fraction in its lowest term.

$9.00

$18.00

What is 30% of $30.00?

What coin has the same value as 50% of $1.00?

$1.00

30% of $60.00

Which is more: 60% of $60.00 or $30.00?

$16.00 is $\frac{1}{2}$ of this amount: $_____._____

10% of $10.00

popcorn

5

60% of $100.00

$60.00

$16.00

80% of $20.00

peanuts

6

Fun Flap Template

Make your own fun flap!

1 Draw a picture in each corner and label it. Write a number from 2 to 9 in the circle.

2 Fill in your own problems and answers. Use the fun flaps in this book as a guide.

3 Write a challenge problem on each set of lines near the center of your fun flap.